Dedicated to Mandy

Our plans have changed for this Easter

Because Grandma and Grandpa can't fly

So, we decided to go and see them

And soon we'll be heading off into the sky!

"But how will the Easter Bunny find us?" I ask.

My older brother laughs.

"Don't worry," Mommy says, "We'll let the Easter Bunny know."

Daddy says, "Mommy always gets everyone where they need to go."

We're all excited to...

JUMP, HOP
AND SAY

Happy Easter

TO YOU
GRANDMA AND GRANDPA!

A few days later we pack our bags. On the way out I say, "We can't forget our bunny ears!"

"Too late now," Daddy says, "We'll have to wear them!"

We're still wearing them when we're seated on the plane.

Still thinking about how we can't wait to...

JUMP, HOP AND SAY

TO YOU
GRANDPA AND GRANDMA!

We eat our lunch

And listen to some tunes

Then the plane lands and we collect our bags.

We think about packing our bunny ears

But decide not to because we can't wait to...

JUMP, HOP AND SAY

TO YOU
GRANDMA AND GRANDPA!

Dad rents a car, we put all our bags in without delay.

We pick up a few things for Gran and Gramps along the way.

When we arrive
we knock

"Come in," Grandma and Grandpa say as they turn the lock.

We open the door and what do we see

Grandma and Grandpa wearing bunny ears!

And the most beautiful EVER Easter Tree!

"Did the Easter Bunny beat us here?" I ask. Everyone laughs but me...

BECAUSE IT'S TIME TO JUMP, HOP AND SAY

Happy Easter

TO YOU!

WE

EASTER!

Other books in the
Jump Series:
Jump Like a Caribou!
Jump Like a Kangaroo!
Jump at the Zoo!
Jump and Say P.U.!
Jump and Say Boo!
Jump and Say Valentine's Day Is
For Kids Too!
Jump and Look For a Clue
Jump and Say Happy Birthday to
You!
Jump For Everything Blue!
Jump and Say Cock-A-Doodle-Do!

Jump and Squawk Like a Cockatoo!
Jump and Ask Is It Ewe?
Jump and Say There's an Ewww in My Stew!
Jump and Cheer Happy New Year!
More books in the Series Coming Soon!

Other Children's Books:
The Three Boulders
Billy Shakespeare
Billie Shakespeare